3

Turtle:

I cannot swing.

 Bird:

I cannot swing.

 Hippo:

I cannot swing.

 **All:**

We cannot play
with you.

4

5

 **Bird:**
Come and play.
Come and fly
with me.

Monkey:
I cannot fly.

 Turtle:
I cannot fly.

 Hippo:
I cannot fly.

 **All:**
We cannot play
with you.

Turtle:
Come and play.
Come and hide
with me.

11

Monkey:

I can hide.

 Bird:

I can hide.

 Hippo:

I can hide.

 **All**:

We can play
with you.

13

All:
Ha ha ha!
You cannot hide,
Hippo.

Hippo:
Yes, I can.
I can hide
under the water.
I can play
with you!

16